SOUWESTO HOME

JAMES REANEY

SOUWESTO HOME

Brick Books

Library and Archives Canada Cataloguing in Publication

Reaney, James, 1926-
    Souwesto home / James Reaney.

Poems.
ISBN 1-894078-43-8

I. Title.

PS8535.E24S69 2005   C811'.54   C2004-906083-X

We acknowledge the support of the Canada Council for the
Arts, the Government of Canada through the Book Publishing
Industry Development Program (BPIDP), and the Ontario
Arts Council for their support of our publishing program.

 Canada Council Conseil des Arts
for the Arts   du Canada   Canadä   ONTARIO ARTS COUNCIL
                                                            CONSEIL DES ARTS DE L'ONTARIO

The cover images are from photographs of the farmhouse
where James Reaney was born. Photographer unknown.

The illustrations and clip art pieces are by James Reaney.

The book is set in Minion.

Design and layout by Alan Siu.

Printed by Sunville Printco Inc.

Brick Books
431 Boler Road, Box 20081
London, Ontario N6K 4G6

www.brickbooks.ca

30 Years Your
Brick Books 1975–2005

To our two grandchildren

Edie and Elizabeth

Contents

LITTLES

Domus

A frog	A cistern
an attic	a mouse
verandah	snake
doorstep	toad
this room	us
stove	cricket
hearth	*achetes domestica*
couch	dog
chimney	swift
weathervane	wind
cornerstone	baby's shoe
lares	*penates*
outside spells	inside spells
priest	priestess
husband	wife
kitchen gods	chocolate faced chef
brown sugar shaker	egg timer
china corn cob	enamelled
kettle	fire
whistle	quiet
peace	happiness
saucer	cup
broom	dustpan
janitor	janitress

Scripsit

The cow, me cow
Mooed at the moon.
These cows mooed at the moon.
How kind of them
To match her mood

❋

Get rid of this reader, I snapped.
Redd it away.
I will, he replied,
When I have read it

❋

For this title,
Care I not a tittle

❋

I shall-
ow!
Saidle
the Puddle

❋

Fat
Was my fate

❋

Short cuts–
Long cuts?

❋

I deep
    end,
    Said the pond

❋

I went father
    to see my further
And farther still
    to see water & mater

Brush Strokes Decorating a Fan

(a)

In bed at night
I think of you
Downstairs there
In the dark–
Chair, table, cupboard,
Dishes, books, my outside boots,
Dear good things
That wait
Patient-
ly
All night
For me & the morning.
Still there
When I get up
And come down
To you

(b)

A sentence of persons drifts by on Huron Street
now
Which started before dawn, ends only at old
moonrise
With a single last traveller
After midnight long

(c)

O cloud unreachable in air
O icicle in my gloved hand
O water in your cupped hand

(d)

This is a blue study:

I see a blue sky above firs blurred with white
Swipes.
We're all in a big, I think,
Bottle round of pale blue ink

(e)
The Wind
Plays cards with us today
Then flings us down & flies away
To comb across the eyes of girls
Their curls,
And drown us in our boat
O wind, friend of us not

(f)
Some think they stripped me.
I say I threw off stale decency
The better to grip the slippery dragon
Whom I pinned with five nails–
Forever!
I had it that
Upright I fought, spouting christening streams,
Rested, relaxed, shrank down–rose again
Forever!

(g)
Ernie's Barber Salon Near the College.
Mr. Delilah, the Barber,
Cuts a field of hair
In his basement shop
When I duck down to see him
In the fraternity field

Scything away

(h)

Leaves speak all summer ss ss ss ss ss ss
" " " " " " " " " fall ch ch ch ch ch ch
" " " " " " " " " winter
" " " " " " " " " spring .. ..

(i)

H20
My cousin says an element we breathe a lot
Long ago
Also
Married a husband who changed her
To slippery indescribabledrinkable uncatchable

(j)

O dear little babes, crawl quickly away
The Butter Box field in Nova Scotia is after you!

(k)

You dirty "thou" rustler
You've stolen my sex,
Purloined my figurative, miraculous
Jesus

(l)

Dark of the Moon moon
Where are you in the Heavens
This dark starry night?
Shall I find you by missing some stars
Blotted out by the veiled face of a nun
Dimly traced out by earthlight?
When at tomorrow's eventide I see your bright sickle

Shall I still wonder who the night before
Smuggled you unseen across the sky?

(m)
Nubia
Where, twice written language disappeared
And twice human sacrifice returned

(n)
Trapped.
Myriads ex-
ecuted in dinosaur tanks,
Mob of prisoners pounding against
Latex

(o)
The ethicals are
Putting on their overshoulds
Picking up their mights
Wandering the woulds
Prowling for cans
And shalls

(p)
Orchard
First a haw,
Small, red, round.
Next a sour

Red & yellow crab.
Then the Ben Davis,
Scarlet, not ripe until March,
But still, even then,
A hog choker
Which you married to Mr. McIntosh
Who smoothed me to the delicious Courtland

(q)
A curse on the "she" who walked yth
my Larousse Encyclopedia of Moff
From my office

(r)
This is the wee the farmers fare out & pic up
stones.
Yes, but why have you left out the Ks?
The Ks are the stones

(s)
In a chapter of the Bell
I met that learned enharmonic novel-
ist
Ding Dong!

(t)
You tore my Jesus from his lake
But put no nymph back,

Only a scum
Petroleum

(u)
A Useful List:
Hermes
Hera
Apollo
Zeus
Venus
Vulcan
Mars
Athena
Vesta
Hades
Poseidon
Ceres.
Useful for what?

Well, I don't quite know yet,
But I swear that as an infant,
Born near the Little Lakes,
I met them.
Every morning in our house,
Vesta used to light the stove

(v)
The hand of my ear
Picks up a distant bell

(w)

I know a book that opens up people
And reads them,
Spreads them out, pleat by pleat,
Till they see as far up as up,
Till they see farther far than down.
It makes so sharp their eyes
That East or West
They can spot Nobody coming up the Road

(x)

I know an experience
That brings my 2 butterfly wings
Tight together
Then open
Now shut
Dull blur
Sudden bright.
Over the years our selves
Have been blended
By all this together,
Pleated & unpleating,
Opening & closing,
Tight together,
Loose apart–
Two sides of a breath

(y)

Sick, I came to my sister's abbey for refuge.
My outlaw forest outside her ruled windows.

In white, she now stands over me
Drinking my blood with sharp lancet.
Satisfied, she waits for my finish.
But my horn she has overlooked
Which I blow upon to summon John
Who brings me my great bow.
It defies her with an arrow
Shooting up & far over my forest
To where I must be buried
There to grow again:
New forest, new merry ways, new story

(z)
Up a walk into a house
I ran
They put me in the stove
Out its chimney smoke
I rose
Into Heaven's Love

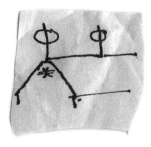

Little Lake District (Where I was Born) Poems

Bells' Corners
Filled with white gray pasturing clouds
Is the big green field of my people's village.
Their wives spin these sheep into flannel,
Clothing from a green field at the crossroads,
One to New Hamburg, one north to Amulree
Foreverly

Roberts' Clayhole & Brickyard
From my pit
Came jail & court house
Church & post office.
Shelter made they from my slime,
Rows of houses that all rhyme.
Now, cedar stumps, snipe, rain-filled scow,
Water fills my communal source now

I am *Jones' Lake*
(Tho' some call me Paff's)
I undertake
With mud
Something more elegant
Than to make a prison–
I drowned a hapless circus
Elephant

I am *Paff's Pond*
And into me I yawned
A suicidal tramp.

Ruth remembers his shoes
Hanging at her father's back door

McPherson's Pond
Every winter
With shallow Gorgon glass
Holds up school
Children skater-skinter

Of *Kirk's Lake*
Back in the bush,
Secret, unknown,
There is no story.
Why should happy
Larches worry?

McCarthy's Lake
Grand Trunk
Railway engines
Drink drank drunk
From McCarthy's smooth bottomless
Glass.
A floating bridge
Accepted as toll
Seven waggons & their teams
And had as ghosts, a black pig,
A drowned Irishman.
And on sunny days, this bridge,
Over the biggest of the Little Lakes,

Was a comfortable pillow
For many big water snakes

Huron Road
In all its straight surveyed push
From Wilmot to Goderich
The Old Huron Road curved only once,
Defeated by the Little Lakes
With their hemlock swamps
Bottomless
Where they bent him south & then north
And caught, therefore, in their crooked snare
Painters & poets, storytellers, eccentrics
Who were born & lived & died there

BIGGERS & BIGGIES

Elderberry Cottage

's windows, last night, rain wrote upon,
And Bobdog, while we slept, was miles away,
Beating the bounds, our frontier nose-spy
Reporting back at dawn.
We reward him for knowing about
Quarrels in lover's lane,
Thieves on the prowl and other such
Nightwalkers.
Canny protector, I pray you:
Bark always when strangers come nigh.
Yes, we cannot smell trespass
Nor hear it, as you can.
Piss a ring of fire round our house,
Our curtilage, my land, my concessional lot.
Lead me safely at last
Under this township to my last cot,
And when Elderberry is a ruin,
Guard my grave from the academic wolf,
The curious professor
With his fine wire-brush
Who would dig me up again
From my happiness, your kingdom.

Senex

An old man getting out of the bathtub
Whose feet are gryphon's claws,
Hears his grandchildren skipping
Outside.
Caught in the glass over the washbasin
Could that ageing satyr
With dangling genitals
Wrinkled & sagging,
One day with wand erect have produced
Those shrieks, that glitter
On his back lawn
Under the shade of the catalpa trees?
Could this lonely limp fish, that–
A mere sprat–
And those two crusts of scrotal dough,
Have saved thousands from nothingness?
The answer, apparently,
Is
Yes!

The Wild Flora of Elgin County

On the roadsides & verges, ditches, ponds, & streams
Of Elgin County,
There are more than 100 families of green persons.
So say those wise guides to the *Flora of Elgin County*,
Messrs William G. Stewart & Lorne E. James,
Of St. Thomas well remembered.
E.g., they invite you to meet Miss Buttercup,
Of the Crowfoot family.
She has a brother named "Cursed Crowfoot"
Who lives in a wet ditch at Kipp's Corners,
Concession V, Yarmouth township.
Miss Buttercup, by the way, lives on a dry clay roadside
And her first name is "Common."
Relatives are Miss Hepatica Americana,
And the Windflowers who live at Carr's bridge,
Two miles south east of Sparta.
Calpa, Miss Marsh Marigold, again at Kipp's Corners,
Stands in peat in the water of a ditch,
And the Red & White Baneberry girls can poison you–
Over in dry sandy Springwater woods.
Now, William Blake says that plants & trees,
That–in other words–"Flora" are
"Men & women seen from afar."
So all these plant families are people,
People you should know,
And become more serene & thoughtful
In doing so.

Tell Us, *Tellus*

O Earth, how do you do,
You Old Round Raft,
O How do you do it?
You lean backward & it's win
Ter
And someone taught you too
To Lean forward & it's Sum
Mer,
You big round fearsome ball
OON!
So very light you float
And yet
So heavy you are–
Tons, tons, tons, tons!
Filled with a mysterious sting,
A power string
That fastens us all to your sides
But makes me sometimes fall
Downstairs when dr
UNK!
And then stay put.
You tubby flashlight battery,
In Baffin Land you have plus
And in Antarctica you have a surplus
Of minus.
So much electric charge,
So much iron
In your Giant Magnet
Core!
How did it ALL COME ABOUT!

Boy, never mind
I spin & spin

A sometimes weary top
With no stop
Perhap
S
I sleep as me & Sun
And my seven or so
Desert sisters
Journey where?

To Where Herself.
One day, the four big rocks within me,
Giantess sisters, giant brothers, they
Will reach the kingdom
They were exiled from
When you have finished embroidering
Shirts for their massive dirts,
Shirts
Made out of the finger prints
Of Time's Whirlwinds,
And,
I will that day see them, find again
The golden chess pieces in the grass
Of a still, awful place
Filled with a dreadful peace.

The Fan

A girl spent all day pleating a fan.
Either we have Verdun & Kursk
Or we have herbivorous people
As the she above
Who spend all day in their garden
Watching butterflies
Or playing with a kite
Or cutting out coloured paper
For a fan
Or a kite
Or balancing the reds of zinnias with those of
amaranths,
For example that plant called Love Lies Bleeding.

I saw a field of men playing football
With a criminal's head.
I saw a field of sunflowers wiped out
By ten thousand tanks.
I saw Aunt Marjorie's paint brush
Destroy a knight in armour
And even a villainous peasant!
I saw our hockey player break a Russian player's
ankle!

And I saw the Fan! giant in the sky
Huge, winnowing!
I saw an armoured car drive up
To arrest an artist
Who was accounted hopelessly a- and un-political
Because he painted nothing but flowers & mice,
But of course was suddenly seen

As the most dangerous rebel in the republic.
And I saw the Fan – big, winnowing,
Make a rhapsody of a windy day,
Separate wheat from straw just like that,
And blow giants & battlefields like dead leaves away!

The Duck

I

Green grass & white duck,
Orange & yellow beak,
Orange & yellow feet.
White stands out plump!
Quack! in the fresh brown pond.
Heads down now in underwater castle!
Up now! floating with duckling passel.
Floating Simpletons,
In Air Court, Water Castle, Sun Ladder,
Please! Surround me with your vision.

II

By the river, just above the dam,
In front of the public changing rooms,
And a beach brought from a kame,

A crowd of grassy idlurious are standing
Watching thro' average secular prisms
Our Evangelical Church's baptisms.

Still in his shoes & his best suit,
Reverend McLeod
Steps into the river.

Come now his would-be followers
Of Jesus: in their best clothes–
White shirts, white shoes, white dresses,

Burgers & burgesses burgeoning last progresses

Of Pilgrim's Progress into Jordan
In their minister's New Jerusalarms.

They reply to his query, "Yes, an orange Yes!"
And he dips them down
While the whole town
Stands curiously dry.

Let us take St. Paul at his word
When he compares Noah's Ark to baptism.

Look at that large working duck-man;
He tars his bottom
He draws up his drawbridge,
Shingles his hair against the long rain,
And dives into the arms of his minister
Like a good monster, into the grip
Of Reverend McLeod, who holds him under
For a forty day water trip.

Down in Water Castle he's concentrating
And jammy crystallizing
All his two-by-two heart, thought, & flesh
Animals!
Such as the tigers of procreation, the elephants
Of work, the hippopotamus of birth,
The dove of life, the raven of death.

Afterwards, in the sun-laddered bath house,
Taking off his wet, puddly clothes,
He seems an ordinary man.
I can see he was born, I see he will die.
He can, & has, reproduced himself, he can

Produce himself, but then I see

He's not a man, but a babe in a new world
Whose tiger hills chaos not just red blubber,
Whose river-horse is a bouncing ball,
Not a monster; whose elephant plays,
Not drudges; whose raven will never
Come back; whose dove carries back the twig of Life,
And whose head is a round rainbow.

O floating, naked simpleton,
Ridiculously pure,
Dock now thy rainboat,
You baptized Jordan swimmer,
Dock it now on my Armenian mountain head,
Ararat!
So I beneath you
May *understand* thee!

The Ship

Out of trees was I made, Oak & Elm.
Up in Canada strong men were sent
To search for, cut down & trim
A four century pine for my mast,
For the unbreakable bow
Of my white wings' electric
Energy-string.
At first when they launched me,
From the cold & salt water I shied
Still thinking & dreaming
Rain water forest thoughts,
But soon I could not live
Without
The sea's wet.
At first, cross with the currents & tides
Pulling me, pushing me,
That lifted me this way & that,
With your help
I learnt to give in to their love.
All the trees in me became
One tree
Who belonged to the sea.
So well had they sawed me, planed me, curved me,
They who for centuries had reckoned the gives,
The gives & the takes
Between wood, wind, water
Between artefact & waterflow,
Starsay & air-go.

To contest with another such was I bred.
Carved she was in a foreign place south of us.
By no means lacking in gold, her builders.
You were chosen my master.

I, swan-winged with fish-arrow body, I
Obeyed your lightest of touches.
We grew to be one
And race after race we won.

Once at Ile-aux-Sables, the graveyard of many
Dunked sailors, sunk ships,
Trapped one whole night
In a sandy cross-currented inlet,
We fought entrapment & embayment,
An uncombable tangle of purposelessnesses
Which, by a whisker, freeing us at dawn,
Having sent your crew below deck,
You solved.
So complete was our love for each other,
One mind, one heart, one corps,
Your sail-thoughts I was & your heart-rig,
Your man-rudder.

At length, I grew old. Heartless the men
Who dismissed you, knotted my sails,
With an engine infested me.
To Hispaniola I carried dried fish,
Fetched back rum & brown sugar,
Fish south, rum north, back, forth,
Year after year,
Until the place to the south
Thinking to defeat us at last
Us again challenged with a new boat
Trimmed with brass, mahogany polished,
Newly wed, strong, young.

Through rough loveless usage, I'd grown
Derelict, cracked, rheumatic,
Shabby & old.
Still, scorning her varnish & modern,
With my sails I hissed at my rival,
For once more I felt your step & touch.
Once more beneath your thigh I rode
So that all through me flew a lightning,
A jump fluid driving us forward,
For you alone recklessly sailing
Swifter & faster than
Any winged ship ever had sailed.
By seamiles we won at the finish line,
As my breaking & splintering then
Came too late to rob us of the win.

Never saw you again.
Mast felled, sails sold, putt-putt
Engine rattling my bones,
With a load of used cars & trucks
Off Haiti I sank
Down to the shark's consolations & coral.

When at the harbour whose yards were my mother
They woke you & told you this news
Of my death while you slept,
I hear, I know that you broke down,
And that, publicly, you wept.

Outside = Inside?

They
Say
We bear in just one cell of us
A sentence marvellous
1,000,000 miles long
Coiled of 3 million letters
To every millimetre–
The Bible for our cell society, for
Blue eyes, 5 fingers, think tank fishes.

Now look up at the night sky
See
That same sentence stretch,
A Milky Whey?
Over the cedar trees
And our long lane.
From Scorpio to the Twins to Virgo
Is
Just
One cell,
A universe!
In you/of us
Outside you, inside of us.
Strange prism prison
Jailed in the prisoner.

Maps

To go where I first saw maps
Is almost too simple perhaps.
Find Pork Street or Hessestrasse
And come up McKone's sideroad past Cardwell's
Till you hit Elmhurst School
Where time is reckoned by a Pequenaut clock
Manufactured in Kitchener, alias Berlin.
And space is taught by gray green windows
Unrolled from their special "map" cupboard
And hung upon the wall with us looking up
At continents Mercatorized,
Anything British vermilionized,
With funny stripes for Palestine
And Egypt, Iraq, Persia and Danzig,
Places only half imperialized,
Or spheres of influence;
However, just over the map cupboard,
Was a wall of continuous windows
That contained my uncle's fields,
When school was over
Basically my way home landscape.
It was a map too!
Its scale was an inch to an inch,
A mile to a mile.
There was no map to guide me home
Save *this* one and a path.
Teaching itself, white with snow, gray sky,
Blurred tree sticks, ditch, swamp,
Forest, meadow, yard, home.
Inside my school – the whole world
In a round globe, or flat maps;
Outside our school – a part of the world
Too big to be taught.

"White Grumphies, white snow..."

The students of Agricultural Diploma, their fathers
Grow square miles of blue flowering flax near
Pilot Mound and square miles of yellow mustard which
I saw as I drove out from Minnesota,
Well knowing that in the fall, in the autumn,
We would be teaching them Robert Penn Warren's
Understanding Poetry, Austen's *Pride and Prejudice*,
Somerset Maugham, Joseph Conrad, Emily Dickinson.

As I climbed the stairs to their classroom
Over the Rupertsland Agricultural Auditorium,
Prepared to teach them "I heard a fly buzz when I died,"
I heard them splitting desk into kindling
For a bonfire in a waste paper basket where they
Burnt the texts on the course one by one.
Rainbow-coloured poems and prose they burnt,
Book by book, as I taught them.
As verbal virgins they were tougher
Than such pastoral nymphs as Diana or urban ones
Such as Athena.

However, a day or two later, taking a random stroll
Across the winter campus, I saw,
Around the corner of the Swine Barn, a herd
Of white, white pigs being driven into the barn
By my Aggie Dip students each with
A very proper and even beautiful pig-driving stick.
Was it their mid-term test in pig herding?
It must have been.
The whiteness of the piggies against the whiteness of the snow
Presented them with optical problems.
They had trouble seeing me as well.
In fact not one of them did, for I
Was wearing this poem.

The Congress Café

At the Congress Café in Austin, Texas,
A group of men & women came in,
Workers in some state office.
They ordered drinks, then meals.
After just twenty minutes,
You could hear the drink they'd drunk
Suddenly, happily, speak out in them.
This sound of community went on until we left.
I have no doubt that afterwards
The drink they had taken
Coupled some of them in matching ecstasies
On Murphy beds.

How many things seek their voice in us?
Unsuspected demons & angels
Wait for the arrangement we provide
Of gut, enzyme, funny bone, nervous system, mind.

Blood we lost long ago?
(On Frederick's great battle field
When first he conquered Angria)
Seeking to recirculate once more?

The apples of the orchard young Elmer Scheerer's
    Father planted
Which his son pressed into cider barrels, then drank
Which then became his wild mouth organ music
Played from a Pippin tree top, or (husband) on wilder
    bed spring,
Printing press of his sons, Stanley & Geordie,
Early friends of mine,
O Congress Café.

Department Store Jesus

May I help you? You want a Jesus?
We have a different style for each of our four
Floors, for
Example, in the basement we stock the demonic Jesus
With the hardware & the mousetraps & the col
-chicum bulbs & the rat poison.
Demonic Jesus, yes–
As portrayed in Martin Scorsese's film where Christ giggles,
An efficient young carpenter apprenticed to his dad,
Helps his father make crosses for the Romans to use.
As portrayed in a Handmade Film bankrolled by one of the Beatles
He says: "Blessed are the Cheesemakers"
And his much more attractive rival is a well-endowed male,
Amiable, but not too interested in changing the world,
Named Brian.

Now, let's take the escalator
To the First Floor where you may prefer
Christ as He really was,
Classified with Kodak film, notions, perfumes,
Stationery & Men's Wear.
This historical Jesus is made up of verifiable only facts,
Of which there are practically none;
Do you know there is a serious doubt that he even existed,
But finding his grave would help.
They've just found that of Caiaphas, the Chief Priest of his time.
The archaeologists are busy.
Water-walker, speed baker & fisher? Virgin birth?
We've scrubbed him clean of all that midrash rubbish.
After all, can you cure leprosy, blindness, & death
That easily?

Meanwhile, a monastery in Turkey has coughed up
A rather interesting Gnostic scrap with regard to
A hitherto obscure passage–Mark IX: 51,52.
At last our suspicions about his sexuality may be–
Explained.

Let us take the Elevator to the Second Floor
Where the Christ of the creeds & the New Testament
Is still available
(Buyers, not many lately)
Among the patterned china, the records for gramophones,
The furniture & dining room suites.
Now this model was born to a Virgin, raised the dead,
Often corpses not so recently deceased,
Bent reality with his magic, died,
Then, like Snow White came alive again:
Dared to be a crucified wretch on cross;
Somehow destroyed & renewed a large empire,
Is, no doubt, our only hope for translating us out of here.
But, you know, we get a lot of returns
And customers asking for something really true this time,
Not so exciting & poetic, more real.

A man who walks on rain
Is too great a stretch for their brain.
Others say they are more than happy, but you can tell
They're not by the funny look in their eyes,
And, of course, we provide a booklet, one of many,
Just in case your difficulty is, say, the Ascension,
Speaking of which, let us climb these stairs

Up to the roof of this Department Store.

On the roof of this Department Store
Having a cigarette on his break,
I saw a young floorwalker
Leaning against the elevator shaft.
By the sudden flash, I recognized Him,
Yes, by the moment glimpse
Of the nailmarks
On His hands.

Entire Horse

Poems Written About The Donnellys To Assist
The Renewal Of The Townhall At Exeter, Highway #4 *

I
Around Borrisokane, in Eire, the roads twist
After cowherds with willow gads, after wise woman's spells,
After chariots and the widest go-around found in a mare's skin.
But in Biddulph, Canada, in Mount Carmel's brooder stove, St
  Peter's fields,
The roads cross at right angles, a careful Euclidian net, roods, rods
Spun by surveyors out of Spider stars – Mirzak, Spicula, Thuban,
  Antares.
Like serpents, twitchgrass roots, dragons – the Irish roads twist,
The old crooked roads twist in the cage of the straight new.

II
We were horsemen, dressed well and from my brother's entire horse,
From his entire horse came the colt fast fleet hoofhand with which
We seized and held onto the path through Exeter down to London.
We lifted the hills, creeks, rivers, slaughterhouses, taverns,
We lifted their travellers and those who were asleep when we passed
And those who saw us rattle by as they plowed mud or whittled.
We lifted them like a graveldust pennant, we swung them up and out
Till they yelled about wheels falling off, unfair competition, yah!
And we lie here now – headless, still, dead, waggonless, horseless,
Sleighless, hitched, stalled.

III
As the dressmaker hems my muslin handkerchiefs,
The night the Vigilantes burnt down one of their own barns,
As I sit waiting for a cake to bake and my gentle niece with me

---

* Respectively, the three speakers of these poems are William Porte, the
  Lucan postmaster, Tom Donnelly and Mrs. Donnelly.

I realize I am not doing what you want me to do.
You – bored with your Calvinist shoes chewed to pieces
By streets of insurance, streets of cakemix, packages, soap,
    sermonettes.
You want me to – you project a more exciting me on me.
She should be burning! Clip! Ax! Giantess! Coarse, I should curse!
Why should I accept these handcuffs from you?

Moses

Was a young stutterer filled with fire
He found so hard
Clearly to utter.
Cumulus he was,
Cumulus cloud 9 miles high
Crushed into a short shepherd
Hiding out in the desert
(He'd murdered a man, an Egyptian)
And he stared at a bush
Until it began to burn & crack to him,
Till it smoked in his tongue
Such words of power
He humbled Leviathan
Who oped his jaws
And let go of this young stutterer's people.

In the desert they starved,
But he found them bread.
When they thirsted,
With God's Wand,
Neither wet nor dry,
He knocked water out of dry rock.
Unlettered they came to Sinai
From which he descended with an alphabet.
Until, yes, at the very last he alone
Was forbidden to enter the garden
He had brought them to.
From the desert side of the river
He stared, still uncircumcized, at it,
He a cumulus cloud 9 miles high
Compressed into a shepherd—
He looked & he died.

The Birth of a Pome

Wanna read a poem, no libraries close by?
First find a poet, then find her a muse.
For a poetess,
God bless,
A male inspirer should not refuse.
Yes, she might,
With reason
In due season,
And, upon reflection
On the best for her selection,
Yes, she might a male inspirer choose.
Later, their baby'll be a poem!

Hurry home
Against the wind
With a poem
On your mind.
Find a quill,
Where's the ink?
Bottle full,
Please don't spill.

Here's the subject, no the object,
Of what this Poet has in mind.
Down on your knees & pay attention–
Yes, yes, wait, wait for inspiration.

You want to write a poem for friends' amusement?
Or just your solitary own?
Or, it's like breathing, ye
Can't stop doing it?
Or very shyly–

It's something you would like to write
Not just for unpaid publication,
But
Even maybe
A poem baby, just think–
To be paid!
To be paid cash
For a poem once inside you, now outside
And published to be read
Perhaps–oh gosh!–in *Fiddlehead*!

Well. Simple task to find some paper,
Sweep some space in the body's attic
By which I mean what's called our brain.
Now, twiddle out the mental static,
And ready you are to write a poem, but
Says she
To we,
"I can't get started in my garret.
Where's my muse? Asleep as usual?"
Yes, madam, all alone in his mountain hut,
Drowsy on his mattress hay,
Il fait la grasse matinée!

"Hey, Muse, today you marry!"
"Nothing doing," snores the jerk!
Tempt him with the bride's great beauty?
He seems to think it's too much work!
So, rave of her face so fair, her bosom hilly?
"When I last saw her," he replies,
"Pancake flat was she – pretty?
Don't be silly!"

We reply with double entendre, suggestive slant,
And what is more
We say she's about to be buried!
At this he raises his head.
"She's called Lenore."
He gets out of bed;
"She'll soon be dead,
Yes, she's just about to die!"
He laces on his boots, oh why
For those whose job 'tis to inspire rime,
Does that get them every time?

Through wind & wet
Back to the garret
To tell our poet,
But there to find
She's gone with the wind!
She's come to harm,
She's gone to the barn
Tempted by a free verse stable boy
Who's also postmodernist,
And also, up in the haymow,
Even now,
By an old tramp extremely uncouth
And, to tell the truth,
An unshaved, rampant literary theorist!
Reminding her that it is
Not a treatise
But a poem we're in,
Let's wipe philosophy off her chin.

Re the wedding ceremony text
Have a talk with groom next:

My advice?
Bridegroom, italicize
Where it says,
Oh emphasize
In particular, your groomship,
To wors-
hip her body with yours!

Now, tell the cook to bake
A higher cake
Fetch a match for the wedding candle,
Also a strong best man with chain & club,
In case the groom is hard to handle.
Where's the ring? The church is full,
Here she comes all dressed in tulle!

Ceremony & reception over
Bride & groom, muse & author
Retired for a night
Of happy delight,
Confiscate all birth controls.
What's that sound of beaten tin pails?
The charivari!
The shivaree!
Crowds of locals intent on beer
What an unpoetic tribe!
Serenading with rattle, drum, & rusty saw,
Which Inspiration might outlaw!
'Tis near the break of day
Before they go away!
Nine months later,
I return with perambulator:
Now a metaphor, now a simile.

Now a leg & some synecdoche,
Trochaic heart & tiny little
Fingers beating out a punchy dactyl.
One line at a time–
Arm rhymes with arm,
Finally, the dear little head
Promises something to be read.
Tho' midwife frowns in woe
That sound as yet is no.
Midwife grabs the baby's leg
Whirls it over her wise old head:
"Whaaaaah! Whaaaaaaaah! Wha aaah!"
No poem better can there be
Than the first cry of newborn baby.
With a self-addressed, stamped return envelope
Put the new born in her cradle
And hope
For acceptance
By all those able.

Don Quixot de la Verismo

Once, *auf Kanada*, I met
A different kind of Don Quixot.
Instead of collecting romances,
He owned several hundreds of realistic novels!
Many copies of James T. Farrell,
And many many copies of Theodore Dreis-
er, illustrated, non-illustrated,
All bought with zeal never sated.
As for Émile Zola–ooh lala, Zoo la la–
His collected works piled on a sofa!

Now this Don Quixot went on a quest
To find nothing of particular interest,
But just to let the environment
Over him be absolutely dominant.
He tried hard not to have adventures,
And talked to people mostly of their dentures.
Until he saw one day
Beside his highway
Giants lined up on the hills.
He thought they were windmills!
And would they grind some flour for him
And fill his water pail to the brim?
Oh, these giants with their giantesses
Of windmills were quite the antitheses.
When he climbed up to them with pail and bag of wheat
Hoping to get something to drink and eat
These giants with terrific ease
Tore him to pieces!
Oh tale of woe!
Another victim of *verismo*!
Don't forget he had a Sancho Panza

Who lagged behind him like a second stanza
And kept telling him they weren't windmills,
"We live in a fairy tale, not in 'real-life' novels!
The Brothers Grimm are right
Dreiser, Farrell and Zola ain't!"
Don Quixot's squire scampered off with a wail,
But not without the wheat and the pail,
Deserting this highway for a nearby wood
As fast as he could!

Descartes

At the top of a lonely house
Lived a philosopher, lived all alone
Chewing on a methodological bone
His only companion, an ill-fed mouse.

Not quite alone, for in the basement
Kitchen lived his cook & all-sorts:
"For you," said she, "I make soup that smacks,
I go to confession, get penance whacks.
My children work in a cotton factory,
One small one lives here with me."

The farmer who brought in food to the cook
Just happened to've read the philosopher's book:
"He says, Sarah, that 'I think; therefore I am.'
About us he seems to give not a damn!"
The farmer went home & refused to stoop
Over the vegetables he grew, unpicked;
Also the cook stopped making the soup
And slept on her bed so well feather-ticked.

Crawling downstairs to see what was up,
The philosopher found nothing to sup.
The cook's child told him to go pick some berries
As she had; his eyes were too weak
To find any; his mind could barely think!

He could not talk!
But he took a piece of chalk
And on a wall
Did he scrawl
For the cook & the farmer to see:
"Yes, I eat; therefore I be!"

Finger Games

My Aunt Letitia–
Making churches with your two hands, fingers
Brought together with Index Finger Steeple
And Thumb Doors.
Aunt Tishy,

You called this a courting game
And could with these same hands
Make a pig stable too,
The little finger pigs madly feeding
At their palm trough.
Dear Aunt
What happiness you taught.

A Field of "Corn"

This field of maize which we call "corn"
In rows & rows
Waits to be shorn, cut & torn.
Green soldiers are you
Rustling to each other,
Grown by the sun
Waved by the wind, an army
Of casualty
At Somme & Verdun.

Janitor

I love gateways into farms & yards: even more
Do I love door-
ways (latches, their hooks, hinges, keyholes).
From my collegiate days
I remember the janitor,
Mr January,
Who lingered, with his blizzard broom
At the highschool's entrance, tending
His garden of galoshes, rubbers, boots,
Mudmats, sleet mops, rainwhisks.
Awesomely quiet, brooding, puttering man,
He had, in his pockets, keys for all locks
Of classroom, gymnasium,
Even the mysterious cubby holes under stairs,
And the exits & entrances of the assembly
Auditorium.
You shuffler & sweeper who opened, who shut,
Kept the rain, wind, mud, snow out,
And us, inside, warm & dry.
Doorkeeper, in some strange way,
You caretaker, though you were
Neither principal nor teacher,
You secretly governed the school.
We often dreamt of you,
Our most remembered educator.

Film Credits

Your name when you worked as cashier
At the Clothing Store.
    Was Sadie Buhl.
Even so named were you, you'll
Remember, in the lists of extras
For crowd scenes in filmodramas,
Until one day you were seen
    By a productive varlet
    As a potential starlet.
With the springs of the casting couch
Still tattooing your back with ouch,
They thought you'd have a better chance
At stardom
If they changed your name.
A toss-up between Sylvia Sonnet
And Vivienne Romance!
He chose the latter
And about this new star in the cinematic sky
Fanatic fans soon were–"crazy."

Now some who went to bed with Vivienne or Syl-
via, woke up, of course, with Sadie Buhl.
    Still, there was no escape
To simpler days & cheaper underwear.
    When you ran away & found work, real work,
    In a small town dress shop, using your old name,
        They hired detectives to winkle you back
            And be a film star again.
        To be a child of the camera shutter.
This morning, I walked by the Bijou Cinema.
   Your show was over & the marquee boy
        Tossed your photo in the gutter.

Lichen

You licker of precambrian rock
I am your liker.
You are both plant and sister
To yeasts, moulds, rusts, mildews.
Hungry for green.
No stems, leaves, nor roots
In you are seen
And so
You married yourself to a plant,
Green plant wed to greenless you,
And together you chew, chew
Rock into earth,
Precambrian into postcambrian,
Helped, no doubt
By the sun and her daughter,
Water.
O determined soil-maker,
We all lie in the hammock
Of your ceaseless patient work.

One Stone

When I was little my uncle said to me:
"Come and play algebra with me.
We'll hunt the x deer through the forest of numbers."
All by myself I've pursued God thro' the stars,
Made equations for energy, fought the dragon of chance,
Made laws for randomness, grew famous by it.
My sons never saw me. Yes, when I was eighteen,
I came to the edge of the forest of numbers,
Escaped for a few nights that forest's beast,
Who soon pulled me back. Now, I come out of my cell,
My wife has died in her sleep, I come out of my house,
There is no world left.
The use they have made of my equations levelled it.
Horizon to horizon, the earth has become
One stone.

Lot

Parking Lot's wife looked back
At the burning vehicle
From which
We had escaped.
In a flash
She turned into a car.
Are there not better gods
Than hot rods?

Ice Cream

The local poet is riding his bike up town
On a fairly hot summer day
Bent on Jumbo's Ice Cream booth
Before mailing a poem to *Chimaera* at the Post Office.
At Jumbo's Ice Cream booth there are
Thirty flavours available including–
Licorice, fudge, lemon, orange, apple, grape,
Banana, chocolate, cherry, Maple Walnut (my favourite)
Vanilla, of course, peppermint, strawberry, raspberry–
Weren't there some vegetable ones? Do I remember–
Onion ice cream?
And this pair of double dip skim milk flavours
Cost only a nickel each!
And the ceiling was of pressed tin!
So, I plunk down a nickel for Maple Walnut!
And so out the door bent on making the cone
Last till I reach the Post Office door–
The Post Office is French Provincial with 4 clocks.
The poet holds his bicycle up with his left hand.
Walks slowly licking as he proceeds.
Two little girls say scornfully: "He's acting
Just like a little kid!"
But he thinks– "Isn't this what life is all about?"

Stage Door

Back in her dressing room
Behind the footlit illusion,
She, on whom
I got a crush tonight,
Takes photonic flight,
And, sharp faced, with a mouth sore,
Is just a flat whore.

As, however, I drink in the noise
Of your haunting voice
No doubt kept by
For young admirers who are shy,
Why,
I lie down on your couch
With its broken springs – ouch!–
Into my neck sticking
And my backside pricking.

Yes, she took this wet puppy in the teeth
Of her sharp face and trotted off
To her den in the strawstack by the barn.
Smelling the smoke from her pipe,
He woke beside her at dawn
Feeling distaste and dislike,
But she spoke:
"You're awake!
Do you still love me now?
This silly old theatrical sow?"

Again, what should have been noise
Turned into silvery voice,
And, as if the moon came out from a cloud,
I said loud,
Forever capable of suspension of dis-
belief, I said, "Yes."

Home Again

After my music lesson
Three miles
Through
The stream
Of wind
And of snow
Of rain & sleet
Tonight
I walk & walk
Till home at last
By stove, hot water, tub,
Supper,
Happy at seeing again my kitchen gods–
The china brown sugar shaker
Shaped like a corn cob
(Cousin Jean gave it to Mother for Xmas)
And her companion on the top of the stove–
The chocolate-faced chef holding
(White chef's hat, white smock cooks wear)
A tiny three minute sand glass
To time the boiling of soft boiled eggs.
Drowsy, listening to radio,
Mother, homework, bed–
There the grateful stream of sleep
Slides in & under
The other stream outside
Still flowing ice & rain.

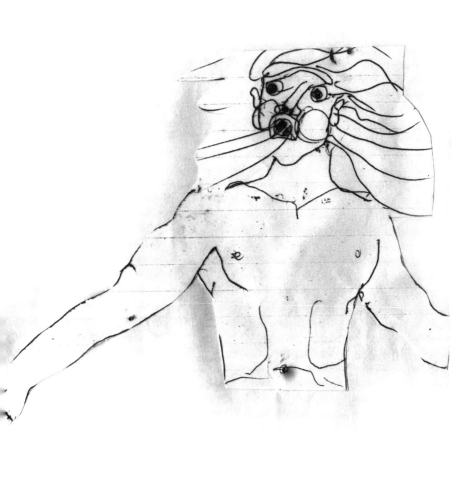

Copyright © London Free Press

James Crerar Reaney was born September 1, 1926 on an isolated farm in South Easthope, near Stratford, Ontario. His parents, Elizabeth Crerar, and James N. Reaney, were interested in theatre and encouraged him in literary interests. From a nearby country school he proceeded to Stratford Collegiate from which he won a scholarship to University College, Toronto where he published poems in the college magazine, *The Undergrad*. His first volume of poems, *The Red Heart*, was published in 1949. By 1951, he was married to fellow poet, Colleen Thibaudeau. They have two children – James Stewart and Susan Elizabeth, and two grandchildren, Elizabeth and Edie. *A Suit of Nettles* followed in 1958, *One-man Masque* in 1960, *Twelve Letters to a Small Town* (1962 and 2002), *The Dance of Death in London, Ontario* (1963), *Poems* (1972), *Imprecations: The Art of Swearing* (1984), *Performance Poems* (1993) and *Two Plays* (2003), the second of which was a new edition of *One-man Masque*. There were, as well, many plays, some in verse, as well as opera libretti with composers John Beckwith and Harry Somers. Honours include The Governor General's Award, won thrice, The Order of Canada, The Royal Society of Canada, and several honorary doctorates.

My editor, Stan Dragland, wishes me to explain "White Grumphies, white snow." They are white pigs herded by agricultural students on a snowy day.

Thanks to Jean McKay, whose assistance has been invaluable.

"The Duck" was recorded for Win Schell's Ergo Productions (www.ergobooks.com), P.O. Box 1439, Stn. B, London, Ontario, N6A 5M2, publisher of Reaney's *Two Plays*.

Thanks to Margaret Atwood for the use of her words on the cover of *Souwesto Home*.

LD-TIME   FIDDLER

REMEMBER HIM?